Winners on the Ski Slopes

WINNERS
ON THE
SKI SLOPES
BY JOHN FRY

A PICTURE LIFE BOOK
FRANKLIN WATTS
NEW YORK | LONDON | 1979

TO MY DAUGHTER, NICOLE

Photographs courtesy of:

Ski Magazine: frontispiece, pp. 6, 9, 10, 36, 38 –
39; *Ski Magazine* and Paul Ryan: p. 40; Suzy
Chaffee: pp. 12, 16; Suzy Chaffee and Colgate
Press: p. 15; Del Mulkey: pp. 18, 20 – 21, 22, 42, 46;
Peter Miller: pp. 24, 27, 28; Hubert Schriebl: p. 30,
33, 34; Swiss National Tourist Office: p. 45.

Cover photograph courtesy of: Del Mulkey

Library of Congress Cataloging in Publication Data
Fry, John, 1930-
    Winners on the ski slopes.

    (A Picture life book)
    CONTENTS: Jean-Claude Killy — Suzy Chaffee
— Sylvain Saudan — Barbara Ann Cochran — Bill Koch
— Nancy Greene — Steve McKinney.
    1. Skiers — Biography — Juvenile literature.
[1. Skiers] I. Title.
GV854.2.A1F79   796.9'3'0922 [B] [920]   78-16443
ISBN 0-531-02292-7

R.L. 2.8 Spache Revised Formula

Contents

Jean-Claude Killy
knows when he skis
fast. He is called
"the man with a
clock in his head."

Jean-Claude Killy

The dream of many athletes is to win an Olympic gold medal. To win all three gold medals in Alpine, or mountain, ski racing is almost impossible. Yet that's what a young Frenchman, Jean-Claude Killy (Zhahn-KLOD Kee-LEE) wanted to do in the winter of 1968.

When he was young, Jean-Claude had learned to ski fast around poles set in the snow. This is called slalom racing. At seventeen, he became a member of the French national ski team. He won the first World Cup of ski racing. Jean-Claude was the most famous skier in the world. But he was thinking of only one thing. "How can I win all three gold medals in the Winter Olympics?"

The Olympics would take place in Grenoble (Greh-NO-bel), France. This was not far from Jean-Claude's home. One week before, Jean-Claude disappeared. Secretly, he went away to rest. He was preparing his mind for the difficult races to come.

The first Olympic race was the downhill. It was steep and terribly fast. It was almost 2 miles (about 3 km) long. Jean-Claude won the race by only the time it takes to blink an eye. It was very close.

When Jean-Claude was a child, he skied every day after school.

The next race was the giant slalom. The giant slalom has more turns in it than the fast downhill. Jean-Claude won it easily. Now he had won two gold medals. There was one more race to go. Just one more medal to win.

The day of the slalom race it was very foggy. The racers had a hard time seeing the poles set in the snow. But Jean-Claude saw through the fog and won. He had done what many people thought could never be done. He had won all three gold medals in Olympic ski racing.

Jean-Claude almost lost his third gold medal. Austrian racer Karl Schranz demanded another chance. But the judges gave Jean-Claude the third medal.

"Skiing should
be graceful
and smooth,"
says Suzy.

Suzy Chaffee

Ballet is usually performed in a theater.
But have you ever heard of ballet outdoors
on the snow? With the dancers performing
on skis?

It all started with a pretty blonde girl
from snowy Vermont. Long before Suzy
Chaffee became a ski ballerina, she learned
to ski with her family. Then she began
racing. Suzy was captain of the American
Women's Ski Team in 1968.

"I exercise every day," said Suzy. "I'm
especially careful about the things I eat.
It's too bad, but most American boys and
girls don't exercise as much as kids in
other countries. I want to help change them
by the example I set myself."

Suzy began to do unusual stunts on skis. She could turn on one ski. Her other ski would be high in the air. She learned to do a full spin in the air. Other skiers, who called themselves *hotdoggers*, could do these stunts. But Suzy added her own idea. She asked for music to be played while she did her stunts. Then she did one after another as she went down the hill. She skied in time with the music. The crowd cheered.

Suzy works hard to get money to improve sports in America. In 1975 she went to the White House to ask for the president's help.

Suzy Chaffee helped to make ski ballet a big sport. Today, it's on television. Girls and women compete for thousands of dollars in prizes.

To be a ski ballerina, Suzy must keep her body in good shape.

*This slope
is very steep.
Huge snowslides,
called avalanches, are a
constant danger for Sylvain.*

Sylvain Saudan

One of the highest mountains in the world
is Mount McKinley in Alaska.

"It was always my dream to ski down
Mount McKinley," said Sylvain Saudan
(Sill-VEHN So-DAN). "It would be the
longest ski descent ever made by man."

Saudan is a climber and skier from
Switzerland. He has skied down many of
the steepest mountains in the world.

To ski down, Saudan needs to make
perfect turns on his skis so that he won't
fall. His body and his legs must be strong.

Saudan needs courage. "If I were
to fall," he said, "I almost certainly would die
because I wouldn't be able to stop myself
from sliding over a ledge or into a crevasse."
A crevasse is a very deep hole in the ice.

One day, in May 1972, Saudan and his friends started to climb Mount McKinley. On the way up, the wind was blowing at 150 miles (240 km) an hour. It took fifteen days to reach the top.

It was very cold at the top. Saudan's ski boots were frozen. He had to use an ax to open the buckles.

Saudan started down in the evening. It was still light, and the snow was like ice. The top part was very steep.

"It took all my courage to make the first turns," he said. "After that I felt confident."

Farther down the mountain Saudan skied around deep, wide crevasses. It was dangerous. Finally, he reached the end. He had skied down a mountain farther than any person before.

Sylvain comes from Switzerland. It is a small, mountain country in Europe.

In faraway Japan, Barbara Ann of Vermont was racing in the 1972 Olympics.

Barbara Ann Cochran

There was one big question in the 1972 Olympics. It was after the first race of the women's slalom. Would Barbara Ann Cochran become the first American skier in 20 years to win a gold medal?

Barbara Ann was a member of the United States Ski Team. It is hard to become a member. Yet three Cochran children were on the U.S. Ski Team! They were Barbara Ann, her sister Marilyn, and her younger brother Bob. Their father, Mickey, had trained each of them to race.

Mickey had found a house in Vermont that had a steep hill behind it. He built a tow to pull the children up the hill. Then Mickey placed poles in the snow.

Barbara Ann, Marilyn, and Bob practiced turning around the poles. They liked to see who could be fastest to the bottom.

"Some days, we would make as many as 800 turns around the poles," Barbara Ann remembers. "We'd practice day after day, every winter."

Mickey also made the children run many miles in the summer. This would make them strong. But no one really had to *make* the Cochrans run. They liked working and skiing together.

Barbara Ann must exercise to keep in shape. She runs even in the cold weather.

At last, the practice paid off. The Olympics began. Barbara Ann won the first slalom run. She was ready for the second run. Two young Frenchwomen had raced before her. She would have to go fast to beat them. Falling snow made it hard to see. Barbara Ann pushed herself out of the starting gate. She was fast. But was she fast enough? She raced across the finish line. Suddenly the crowd roared as her time flashed on the board. She had won. Her brother and sister and other team members put Barbara Ann on their shoulders. Their sister had won a gold medal.

Her hard work paid off when Barbara Ann won the slalom.

*Bill shows his
expert form for
cross-country skiing.*

Bill Koch

Few people in the United States or Canada used to ski cross-country. There were not many people to teach them. To become a champion, a young person had to practice alone. Bill Koch (Coke) wanted to become a champion even when he was eight years old. He lived in a village in Vermont, far from Scandinavia and Russia where the great cross-country skiers lived. In the summer, Bill ran great distances along country roads, alone.

"I work out almost three hours every day," Bill said. "I practice running uphill. Using my poles is very important in climbing hills on cross-country skis. So I work to make my arms strong."

In 1976, no American or Canadian skier had been able to come closer than seventeenth in an Olympic cross-country race. Bill Koch hoped to do better.

Bill's first Olympic race was the 30 kilometer (about 19 miles). It would be tough going up- and downhill for almost two hours.

Bill is the oldest of six children. He practiced for twelve years to become a champion skier.

Bill started out fast. He kicked the tails of his skis high to move himself forward on the snow. He pushed on his poles to go faster. At the halfway point, it looked as if three Russian skiers would win the race. But Bill caught up with two of the Russians and passed them. Sweat poured down his face. He was breathing hard. Exhausted, hearing the crowd's shouts in his ears, he reached the finish.

The race was over. A Russian finished first. But just 28 seconds behind the Russian was Bill Koch. He had won a silver medal. It was the first medal ever won by an American in Olympic cross-country skiing.

Bill catches up with one of the Russian skiers in the race.

The maple leaf on Nancy's
helmet means she is Canadian.

Nancy Greene

World Cup ski races are held every winter, from December to March. The skiers travel to different countries. In each race they can win points. The racer with the most points wins the World Cup. For Nancy Greene, the winter of 1967 didn't end until the very last race.

Nancy Greene was a cheerful young woman. She was just a little over 5 feet (1.5 m) tall. She had made herself strong by exercise. Nancy was from the mountains of British Columbia in Canada. But she had spent most of the winter in Europe. There she raced against skiers from France, Austria, Switzerland, and America.

The last race of the World Cup season was in Jackson Hole, Wyoming. Nancy had to win the last slalom of the year if she was to win the World Cup.

She was confident. "I'm not as big as the other racers," said Nancy, "but I can beat them. I just work a little harder — that's all."

Here is Nancy with Jean-Claude Killy at the 1968 Olympics.

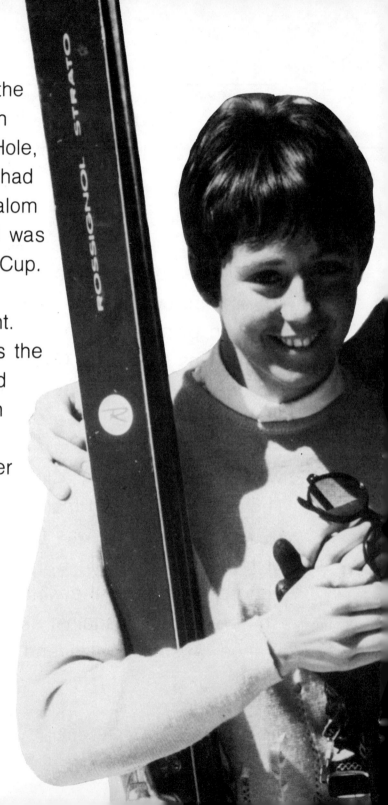

"In the starting gate, I think about the race ahead," Nancy said. "I memorize all the turns. Then, in the last few seconds, before I go, I race it in my mind."

Nancy raced out of the starting gate. The steel edges of her skis made a whining sound on the hard, icy snow. She turned fiercely down the course. With a last push, she raced across the finish line, stopping the clock. It showed she had skied faster than anyone. She had won the World Cup.

Nancy is still the champion of all time. No racer from Canada or the United States has ever won the World Cup again.

Nancy needed to earn 25 points in the race at Jackson Hole, Wyoming. She had to win first place.

*Steve almost rolls up
in a ball on his skis.
This allows him to
go as fast as possible.*

Steve McKinney

High in the Alps of Europe is the famous
peak called the Matterhorn. Just across
from it, an unusual ski race is held every
year. It is not like any other ski race
because the skiers don't turn. Instead, they
aim their very long skis straight down the
mountain. They bend down very low, and
they go as fast as anyone could possibly
go. By 1974, the world speed record on
skis was 114 miles (183 km) an hour. That
was the record Steve McKinney, a 21-year-
old skier from California, set out to beat.

   Steve and his friend, Tom Simons,
arrived early in the summer. The race they
would enter is called the "Flying Kilometer."

The Flying Kilometer is held in summer. That is when the snow high up on the mountain melts and freezes. As a result, it is very fast and very dangerous.

Each day, Steve and Tom practiced. Each day they went a little faster. Finally the day arrived to time the speeds of the skiers. On the first run, Steve, Tom, and an Italian skier were very fast. They all broke the old world record of 114 miles (183 km) an hour.

The Matterhorn is across from the slope where the "Flying Kilometer" is held. The race is very dangerous. A Swiss skier was killed when he fell during practice.